DEVON TRAVEL GUIDE 2025

Stunning Coastlines, Rolling Countryside, and Historic Seaside Towns

COPYRIGHT

No part of this book may be reproduced, distributed, or transmitted in any form or by any means, including photocopying, recording, or other electronic or mechanical methods, without the prior written permission of the publisher, except in the case of brief quotations embodied in critical reviews and certain other non-commercial uses permitted by copyright law.

© [2025] [Nora Atlas]
All rights reserved.

PREFACE

Every traveler's heart and imagination are captured by Devon. It provides the ideal getaway for anyone looking for adventure, leisure, and cultural exploration with its rocky shores, undulating terrain, and classic seaside villages. This breathtaking area of England offers something to attract every tourist, whether they are drawn to the untamed grandeur of Dartmoor, the allure of ancient fishing communities, or the decadence of a traditional Devonshire cream tea.

This comprehensive handbook has been thoughtfully created to help you make the most of Devon in 2025. It goes beyond the typical tourist attractions to find hidden jewels, picturesque itineraries, and life-changing experiences with professional advice, insider knowledge, and current perspectives. This book is your go-to guide whether you're a history buff touring historic sites, a nature lover excited to explore the South West Coast Path, or a foodie seeking for local specialties and fresh seafood.

Devon is one of the most alluring travel destinations in the UK because of its distinctive fusion of bustling culture, rural peace, and seaside grandeur. Every traveler, from first-time tourists to seasoned adventurers, may make the most of their trip with the help of this book. You can easily organize your vacation with the help of helpful tips on lodging, transportation, budgeting, and environmentally friendly travel, and your journey will be filled with memorable experiences thanks to the well chosen suggestions.

Prepare to be taken to picturesque moors, golden beaches, and historic villages that seem straight out of a postcard as you turn the pages. Devon has a way of making every journey memorable, whether you're coming for a long rural retreat or a quick weekend escape.

TABLE OF CONTENTS

COPYRIGHT	2
PREFACE	3
TABLE OF CONTENTS	5
OVERVIEW	6
PLANNING YOUR TRIP	16
TRAVELING TO DEVON	25
NAVIGATING DEVON	34
DEVON'S STUNNING COASTLINES	42
ROLLING COUNTRYSIDE AND NATIONAL PARKS	52
HISTORIC SEASIDE TOWNS AND VILLAGES	60
FOOD AND DRINK IN DEVON	70
OUTDOOR ADVENTURES AND ACTIVITIES	78
DEVON FOR FAMILIES	87
ROMANTIC DEVON	97
ARTS, CULTURE, AND LOCAL TRADITIONS	106
ANNUAL EVENTS AND FESTIVALS IN 2025	117
DEVON'S ECO-FRIENDLY & SUSTAINABLE TRAVEL	127
USEFUL INFORMATION	137

OVERVIEW

Imagine historic seaside towns that have withstood the test of time, rolling green hills that lead to quaint villages, and golden sands that stretch along magnificent coasts. Greetings from Devon, a county whose natural splendor and extensive history combine to make for a truly remarkable vacation. Devon has plenty to offer every type of visitor, whether they are drawn to its breathtaking coasts, picturesque countryside, or lively cultural environment.

Devon, which is tucked away in Southwest England, is special because it is the only English county with two distinct coastlines: one on the English Channel in the south and one on the Bristol Channel in the north. It is an ideal destination for outdoor enthusiasts because of its dual-coastline attractiveness, which allows tourists to take in both soft, sandy beaches and rocky, dramatic cliffs. The inland Dartmoor and Exmoor National Parks are home to ethereal moorlands, historic forests, and picturesque walking paths that transport visitors to another planet.

Devon, however, has a rich history in addition to its stunning scenery. The history of the county is woven throughout, from the Jurassic Coast, which is teeming with fossils, to Exeter's medieval towns. Tiny fishing villages like Clovelly, with their cobblestone streets and ancient cottages, take visitors back in time, while seaside cities like Torquay, Sidmouth, and Ilfracombe offer a beautiful blend of Victorian grandeur and modern charm.

Then there is the cuisine. Enjoying a pint of locally produced West Country cider, fresh fish direct from the harbor, or a Devonshire cream tea are essential components of any Devon vacation. Whether dining at a Michelin-starred restaurant or a small rural pub, the county's booming culinary industry highlights regional ingredients.

Whether you're planning a leisurely beach vacation, an exciting hiking adventure, or a thorough exploration of the local history and culture, this book is made to make sure you have a fun and easy time seeing Devon.

How to Use This Guide

This book is designed to give you all the information you need to make your Devon experience as smooth as possible, from useful travel advice to undiscovered treasures.

Get expert advice on how to plan your trip, how much to spend, and what to bring on your trip to Devon. This area makes sure you're ready for everything, whether you're coming for a weekend or a longer stay.

Discover the most convenient ways to travel to Devon by rail, automobile, ferry, or airplane. To get the most out of your trip, also learn about beautiful roads, auto rentals, and public transportation.

Discover the best of both worlds with Devon's stunning coastlines and rolling countryside, including its beaches, coves, and coastal walks, as well as its national parks, quaint towns, and rural getaways.

Discover the most cherished towns in the county, from the thriving ports of Brixham and Dartmouth to the historic charm of Exeter and Totnes.

Food, Drink, and Local Specialties: Sample Devon's cuisine at the greatest local restaurants, including traditional dishes and fresh fish.

Outdoor Adventures & Family Fun: This book outlines the best outdoor activities for adventurers and families, regardless of your interests in surfing, hiking, cycling, or animal viewing.

Romantic Escapes & Luxury Retreats: For couples seeking a romantic vacation, discover remote beach locations, opulent spa retreats, and the most breathtaking sunset views.

Sustainability & Responsible Travel: Discover how to visit Devon while promoting environmentally friendly lodging, sustainable food, and conservation initiatives for wildlife.

Annual Events & Festivals: Keep abreast of Devon's most significant festivities, including food festivals, cultural gatherings, and outdoor pursuits in 2025.

Practical Information & Travel Advice: Learn important information about prices, currency, emergency contacts, local customs, and helpful apps to help your vacation go more smoothly.

This book is adaptable; you can skip to the parts that most interest you and customize your trip to your tastes, whether you're searching for a comprehensive schedule or simply a few essential suggestions.

What's New in 2025

Devon brings thrilling new events, attractions, and travel opportunities each year, and 2025 is no exception! What is new for this year is as follows:

1. Remodeled Outdoor Areas & Coastal Walks

Along the South West Coast Path, Devon's coastal pathways are undergoing significant renovations that will improve accessibility and provide additional picturesque vantage spots. Additionally, new photography and wildlife-focused guided trips are being launched.

2. Initiatives for Sustainable Travel

With more carbon-neutral hotels, electric bike rentals, and locally sourced dining options, Devon is setting the standard for eco-tourism. Keep an eye out for zero-waste eateries opening up all around the county and new eco-friendly lodging options in Dartmoor.

3. Innovations in Food and Drink

Devon's rich culinary legacy will be celebrated in 2025 with the opening of a number of new farm-to-table eateries, ciderries, and artisanal marketplaces. A Devon Wine Trail showcasing nearby vineyards, interactive cooking classes, and seasonal tasting menus are all to be expected.

4. Historical and Cultural Highlights

Numerous historic locations and institutions are being expanded and restored, such as the reopening of the medieval smugglers' tunnels in Brixham and the recently refurbished Exeter Cathedral visitor experience.

5. Exciting Upcoming Events & Festivals

2025 is jam-packed with events that highlight the finest of regional music, culture, and outdoor pursuits, such as the Devon Seafood Festival and Dartmoor's Adventure Week.

6. Family-Friendly Events & Attractions

Devon is becoming even more family-friendly with the launch of new interactive museums, adventure parks, and animal sanctuaries. Keep an eye out for interactive activities such as boat tours with a pirate theme, farm stays, and fossil digging.

Are You All Set to Explore Devon?

Devon offers a unique experience whether your goal is to relax by the sea, hike through historic settings, or become engrossed in the past. It is a place that lingers in your memory long after you have left because of its breathtaking coasts, undulating terrain, and old seaside villages.

With its wealth of professional advice, local knowledge, and undiscovered treasures, this guide is the perfect travel companion to make your trip to Devon genuinely unforgettable.

So prepare to fall in love with Devon in 2025 by grabbing your map and packing your bags!

PLANNING YOUR TRIP

Organizing your Devon vacation should be thrilling rather than daunting. Your visit will go well and be an unforgettable experience if you are prepared and have the correct information. Here are some crucial pointers for maximizing your stay in Devon in 2025, regardless of whether you're there for the first time or coming back to see more of this stunning area.

Best Time to Visit Devon

Although Devon's splendor is evident throughout the year, the ideal time to visit will depend on your preferences. This information will assist you in determining the best time to leave for this breathtaking county.

March through May is spring.

In Devon, spring is a great time to see the natural world come to life. Hiking and cycling are ideal as the weather warms and the countryside is covered in new greenery. Many gardens and nature reserves start to blossom during this time of year, and if you enjoy wildlife, you'll adore seeing lambs in the fields and birds returning to their nests. Avoiding the summer crowds is best done in the spring, especially at more visited locations like Exmoor or Dartmoor.

June through August is summer.

For good reason, Devon's busiest season is summer. It's the ideal time of year to enjoy Devon's beaches and outdoor activities because of the longer days and milder weather. For those who enjoy water sports, the greatest times to surf, kayak, and paddleboard along the coast are during the summer. Just be ready for an increase in tourists over this period, especially in well-known coastal communities like Torquay and Ilfracombe. This is where Devon really shines, if you don't mind a little more hustle and bustle.

September through November is fall

One of the most charming seasons to visit Devon is in the fall. Particularly on Exmoor and Dartmoor, the fall leaves transforms the landscape into a breathtaking red, orange, and yellow palette. The summer throngs have begun to disperse, yet the weather is still pleasant enough to enjoy outdoor activities.

With so many harvest festivals and local markets throughout the fall, it's also a perfect time to discover Devon's culinary culture. It's the ideal time of year for a comfortable getaway at one of Devon's rustic inns, and the milder weather makes hiking across the countryside particularly delightful.

December through February is winter.

Devon's winters are serene and ideal for anyone looking for a quiet retreat. Cozy cottages and ancient pubs provide a snug haven despite the colder and windier weather in some coastal districts. Christmas markets and regional festivities are a feature of the holiday season, particularly in Exeter and Tiverton. If you're looking for a peaceful getaway or are drawn to Devon's winter moors and coastlines, now is the ideal time to go. Just make sure to check availability in advance because some lodgings can close for the season.

Budgeting for Your Trip

Devon has a variety of experiences to suit every budget, from luxurious beach retreats to reasonably priced country retreats. Here's how to get the most of your trip by carefully planning your money.

Accommodation

Devon has accommodations for every budget, ranging from opulent spa hotels to quaint bed & breakfasts. Staying in tiny towns or villages outside of the main tourist attractions is a good option if you're on a tight budget. You'll discover more genuine experiences and more reasonable costs. Exmouth and Bideford, for instance, provide reasonable value without sacrificing charm or scenic beauty. Consider making reservations for a stay in a cottage or vacation park in the country if you want a genuinely unique experience. There, you may take in the tranquil surroundings without going over budget.

Consuming Food and Drink

There is something for everyone in Devon's varied culinary scene. You may enjoy local cuisine on any budget, from classic fish & chips to top-notch seafood. Visit neighborhood bars, cafes, and farmers' markets for more affordable options. There, you can obtain seasonal, fresh products at affordable costs. There are also several great food trucks and takeout options in Devon. Treat yourself to a memorable evening at one of Devon's Michelin-starred restaurants, such as The Mason's Arms in Knowstone or The Elephant in Torquay, if you want to indulge in a meal.

Activities

Hiking and beach excursions are among the many free or really inexpensive outdoor activities available in Devon. However, some sites, such the Dartmoor Zoo, Exeter's Royal Albert Memorial Museum, or a boat ride along the Jurassic Coast, could charge admission. Free walking tours, neighborhood celebrations, and touring public gardens or historic places are all affordable choices.

Packing Essentials for Coastal and Countryside Travel

The activities you intend to engage in will determine how much you pack for Devon, but regardless of the season, there are a few necessities you'll need. To make sure you're ready for everything Devon has to offer, here is your checklist.

Clothes

clothing: It's advisable to bring clothing because Devon weather can change suddenly. No matter the weather, you can stay warm with a lightweight jacket or fleece for cold mornings, a waterproof layer for sudden downpours, and a few t-shirts and pants for warm afternoons.

Footwear: Sturdy walking shoes or boots are necessary for hiking and experiencing Devon's untamed nature. If you intend to visit the beaches, sandals or flip-flops are ideal for walks along the shore.

Swimwear: It's essential to bring swimwear whether you want to unwind at a spa or take a dip in the ocean.

Add-ons

Even if you're going in the spring or fall, sunscreen and sunglasses are still necessary throughout the warmer months.

Use a camera or smartphone to record the breathtaking views of the coast and the wildlife you come across.

Additional Necessities

If you're coming from outside the UK, bring a travel adaptor.

A first aid kit for small wounds, abrasions, or stings sustained when exercising outside.

Travel Insurance and Safety Tips

Even though visiting Devon is generally safe, it's a good idea to be ready. Here are some crucial travel safety and insurance recommendations.

Insurance for Travel

Before your journey, we strongly advise getting travel insurance. This will protect you against unanticipated events such as medical emergencies, lost luggage, or trip cancellations. If you intend to engage in outdoor activities like hiking, cycling, or water sports, look for policies that also cover these.

Tips for Health and Safety

Drink plenty of water because Devon's outdoor pursuits can be taxing, particularly if you're walking. Have a bottle of water on hand.

Respect wildlife: Always maintain a safe distance and abide by any stated rules if you come across local species, such as birds, seals, or livestock.

Recognize your route: To prevent getting lost when hiking or walking on trails, carry a map or GPS.

You may make your Devon vacation planning as easy or as exciting as you choose. No matter when you arrive or what you have in mind, you can make the most of this amazing place with a little planning.

TRAVELING TO DEVON

Devon is easy to get to and offers a range of picturesque travel alternatives, whether you're coming from the bustling city of London or going from further away. Whether you're traveling by train, automobile, airplane, or even boat, this chapter will walk you through every option for getting to this stunning region of England and offer practical advice for a hassle-free arrival.

By Train: Routes from Major UK Cities

Train travel is one of the most practical and picturesque methods to reach Devon. For those who like to unwind while taking in the countryside, the UK's rail system provides wonderful links to Devon from major towns including London, Bristol, Manchester, and Birmingham.

Devon to London

The easiest method to get there from London is to take a train from London Paddington to Plymouth or Exeter St. Davids. With the quick Great Western Railway (GWR) services, the trip to Exeter, the entry point of Devon, takes around two hours. Before you reach Devon, you'll be treated to vistas of the gorgeous countryside, including the undulating hills of Somerset.

Regular local trains from Exeter make it simple to connect to other areas of the county, such as Torquay, Barnstable, and Paignton. If you want to visit Devon's picturesque coastal towns or national parks, these links are also excellent.

From Bristol

If you're traveling from Bristol, Exeter or Plymouth may be reached in under one and a half hours by Great Western Railway. You get a wonderful sense of the environment before you even reach Devon thanks to the picturesque drive from Bristol, which offers vistas of the Somerset Levels and the Avon Gorge.

From Birmingham and Manchester

You can take an Intercity Express or CrossCountry service if you're coming from Manchester or Birmingham. You will travel through stunning scenery, such as the Cotswolds and portions of the West Country, throughout the around 3.5–4 hour excursion. Before continuing on into Devon, you might need to change trains in Bristol or Exeter.

In the UK, train travel is a great option for tourists who wish to avoid the hassle of driving because it is both comfortable and environmentally beneficial. You'll have no problem arranging a trip to Devon into your schedule because of the regular services.

By Car: Scenic Drives and Road Trip Tips

Driving is the finest way to see Devon, one of those areas that is best explored at your own time. Driving across Devon allows you the chance to find hidden jewels that you may otherwise miss, thanks to the expansive seaside views and winding country lanes.

Devon to London

Take the M4 highway toward Bristol if you're traveling from London, and then follow the Exeter signs. Depending on traffic, this trip will take you approximately three and a half to four hours. The M5 is a simple, well-maintained road with plenty of service stops where you may take a breather.

Once in Devon, you may reach Exeter, the primary transportation hub for the area, via the M5 motorway. The alternatives are unlimited from there: take the A30 to explore the Dartmoor National Park, the A38 to Plymouth, or the A380 to Torquay.

Beautiful Coastal Roads

Traveling by car along Devon's coastline is among the best ways to see the state. The South West Coast Path, which is lined with quaint towns, undiscovered beaches, and rocky cliffs, is a popular tourist destination. From Exeter, head for Dartmouth and Salcombe on the A379 highway. The road follows the coastline, providing breathtaking views of the ocean as well as a peek at Devon's well-known towns and harbors.

Tips and Drives in the Country

Devon's county roads are a haven for anyone who appreciates a tranquil rural trip. Take the A30 via Exmoor National Park, where roads meander through woodland and moorland, providing peaceful vistas of the undulating hills and wildlife. The trip from Tiverton to Dulverton on the B3227 is a lovely, rural route through verdant farmland and delightful villages if you're in the mood for a picturesque detour.

It's crucial to drive carefully and be ready for infrequent single-lane highways because Devon's roads can be small in some spots, particularly in Exmoor and Dartmoor. It's also a good idea to schedule your stops in advance, especially during the summer, as parking can be scarce in some of the smaller seaside towns.

By Air: Closest Airports and Connections

Flying can be a quicker method to get to Devon, especially if you're coming from a greater distance, even though taking the train or driving gives a more picturesque experience. Devon is a great option for foreign travelers because its closest airports provide convenient access to major UK and worldwide locations.

Exeter International Airport

Devon's main airport, Exeter International Airport, is situated just outside the city. Exeter is a fantastic starting point for your Devon experience, with domestic flights from major cities including London, Manchester, and Birmingham, as well as connections to Europe. The Exeter St Davids railway station is only a short taxi ride or a 20-minute bus trip from the airport, providing excellent access to the city centre.

Airport in Bristol

Devon is around a 90-minute drive away from Bristol's airport, which offers a large selection of both local and international flights. You can just take a train to Exeter, Plymouth, or other Devon locations from there.

Other Airports in the Area

Although Exeter and Bristol are the nearest airports to Devon, additional well-connected airports that provide easy access to the southwest region of the UK are Newquay Cornwall Airport (approximately a 1.5-hour drive away) and Plymouth City Airport (mostly for regional flights).

Ferry Services: Arriving from France and Beyond

Ferry services provide visitors from France a thrilling and picturesque way to get to Devon. One of the county's oldest marine cities, Plymouth, is where ferries from Saint-Malo and Roscoff in France dock. It takes roughly six hours to take the boat from Plymouth to Roscoff, and eight hours to take the ferry from Plymouth to Saint-Malo.

Since many boats let passengers bring cars, this is a great method to go to Devon if you wish to bring your bike or car. After arriving in Plymouth, you can travel the rest of Devon by train or by car along the coast.

There has never been a simpler way to go to Devon, and the trip itself is an adventure regardless of the mode of transportation. There are several methods to get to this breathtaking region of England, including by rail, automobile, airplane, and boat.

NAVIGATING DEVON

Getting around Devon is the next step after arriving, and there is something for everyone, whether you're searching for eco-friendly solutions, beautiful routes, or convenience. This chapter will go over all of your alternatives for getting around the county, including walking and bicycling routes, public transportation, and rental cars. We'll also discuss how to make Devon more accessible to all tourists so that your trip is both seamless and unforgettable.

Public Transport: Buses and Trains
Buses

With Devon's well-established and reasonably priced bus system, it's simple to travel about the county at your own speed without a car. Buses can take you to more isolated areas of Dartmoor or Exmoor, or they can take you from Exeter to Plymouth.

The Stagecoach bus business offers frequent services between major towns and cities along a variety of routes throughout Devon. Additionally, there are seasonal bus lines that travel along the breathtaking Jurassic Coast for visitors who like to see the coastal areas. The X53 is a well-traveled highway that connects Exeter, Sidmouth, Seaton, and Lyme Regis, offering a handy way to enjoy the stunning surroundings.

Buses may be less common in more rural or isolated locations, so it's a good idea to check timetables beforehand. Although buses still travel to many of Devon's smaller settlements, they are typically less frequent, particularly on Sundays and in the evenings.

Trains

Train travel is an excellent mode of transportation for large distances. Major rail lines connect Exeter to Plymouth, Paignton, and Barnstable, providing excellent train connections throughout Devon. The Great Western Railway (GWR) runs these routes, which include both regular services and picturesque routes that travel through places like Dartmoor and the coast of South Devon.

With trains traversing the stunning scenery and offering views of the Tamar Valley, the Plymouth to Exeter line is especially lovely. For a more relaxed experience, think about taking a vintage steam train ride along the Dart Valley on the South Devon Railway.

Car Rentals and Driving Tips

One of the greatest ways to see Devon is to rent a car if you want the independence and flexibility that come with driving. With your own set of wheels, you can explore the country's expansive countryside, quaint villages, and coastal cities at your own speed, pausing when something strikes your attention.

Car Rental

Car rental services are available at the airport, train stations, and city centers of Devon's major towns and cities, such as Exeter, Plymouth, and Torquay. When it comes to picking up your automobile, you will have several options because top car rental firms like Enterprise, Hertz, and Avis are available.

It's crucial to reserve your car in advance if you intend to drive in Devon, especially during the busy summer months when demand may be strong. If you intend to travel the winding country lanes and clifftop roads that Devon is famous for, think about renting a small car.

Driving Advice

Although driving in Devon is generally easy, there are a few things to consider, particularly if you're not accustomed to driving on country roads. Always drive carefully and pay attention to other cars because Devon's country lanes can be winding, narrow, and occasionally fairly steep. You'll need to slow down and wait for an opportunity because there might not be much space to pass in isolated places like Exmoor and Dartmoor.

Because the roads hug the cliffs, be ready for steep hills and tight turns if you intend to drive along the coastline, particularly in the area of Torquay or Salcombe. Also, it's important to think about the timing of your trip because traffic can be particularly bad in the summer, especially in the vicinity of well-known beach towns like Paignton or Exmouth.

Parking

In Devon, parking can be difficult during peak hours, especially in cities and coastal towns.

Use park-and-ride lots or public parking lots whenever you can, and be careful to verify local parking laws. These are typically more convenient and reasonably priced.

Cycling and Walking Routes

Devon provides a range of walking and cycling paths that pass through some of the most breathtaking scenery in the UK if you'd rather explore the county in a more environmentally responsible manner. There are routes for all skill levels, from the moors to the seaside path, whether you're a family seeking a leisurely walk or an experienced explorer.

Riding a bicycle

With so many cycling routes that accommodate both novice and expert cyclists, Devon is a cyclist's dream come true. One of the most well-liked cycling routes is the 180-mile Tarka Trail, which runs from Exeter to Barnstable and winds through charming villages, woodlands, and agricultural areas. The path is perfect for a calm ride because it is largely devoid of traffic.

There are many routes along the Jurassic Coast, a UNESCO World Heritage site, along the South West Coast Path for individuals who like seaside views. There are many doable sections of the coast path for families or novice cyclists, even if other sections could be better suited for more experienced riders.

Strolling

Devon has many routes and trails for walkers, ranging from leisurely coastal walks to strenuous moorland excursions. The South West Coast Path, which runs more than 600 miles along the coast and goes through some of the most stunning scenery in the UK, is one of the most well-known walking routes.

The Dartmoor National Park is another excellent choice. There are several walking paths there, such as the Two Moors Way and the Dartmoor Way, which both provide breathtaking views of the moorland and historic stone circles. There are also a number of walking trails on Exmoor, which lead to some of the UK's most breathtaking coastlines and wind through forested valleys.

Accessible Travel in Devon

There are many options for those with mobility issues or other accessibility concerns, and Devon is dedicated to making its beauty accessible to everyone.

Transport That Is Accessible

With low-level platforms and vehicles built to assist passengers with mobility issues, the majority of Devon's public transportation options, including buses and trains, are wheelchair accessible. Private hire services and accessible taxis are also available in Exeter and Plymouth.

Trails Accessible to Wheelchairs

Many of Devon's beautiful bike and walking paths were created with accessibility in mind. There are accessible portions of the Tarka Trail and the South West Coast Path, and several Devon beaches, including those at Exmouth and Torquay, have beach wheelchairs available for guests with mobility impairments.

To ensure that everyone can enjoy this stunning region of the world, Devon's visitor centers and attractions now offer information on accessible paths.

Finding the ideal balance between convenience, excitement, and leisure is crucial when navigating Devon. Devon provides the ideal means of seeing its varied landscapes and quaint villages, whether you decide to walk, cycle, rent a car, or take public transportation. All of these options will make your trip pleasant, easy to get to, and unforgettable.

DEVON'S STUNNING COASTLINES

With their captivating fusion of natural wonders, charming communities, and seaside beauty, Devon's coasts are the county's lifeblood. Devon's coastlines provide something for everyone, whether you're more interested in the rocky cliffs of the North or the broad, sandy beaches of the South. Discover the distinctive coastal landscapes, top beaches, hidden coves, and the South West Coast Path's iconic walking routes as you travel through North Devon and South Devon in this chapter.

North Devon vs. South Devon: A Coastal Comparison

Both North Devon and South Devon have breathtaking coasts, but because of their varied topography and charm, they each provide a different kind of seaside experience.

North Devon: untamed and tough

With its spectacular cliffs, expansive sandy beaches, and untamed terrain, Devon's northern coastline is known for its wild and rugged beauty. For those looking for solitude and adventure, North Devon is the ideal destination. While Croyde Bay and Saunton Sands are well-liked by beachgoers and kite surfers, Woolacombe Beach, with its enormous expanses of golden sand, is a surfer's heaven. Towering cliffs and remote bays border the shoreline, making it the ideal place for a day of exploring.

The Exmoor National Park, which offers stunning views as its spectacular cliffs plummet into the Atlantic Ocean, is also located in North Devon. With its breathtaking rock formations extending above the water, the Valley of Rocks near Lynton is a must-see and offers a genuinely remarkable coastal experience.

South Devon: Calm and Beautiful

The coast of South Devon, on the other hand, is renowned for its softer scenery, quaint coastal towns, and undulating hills that descend to the ocean. These beaches are ideal for families and anyone looking to unwind because they are typically more protected. While Blackpool Sands, close to Dartmouth, provides a peaceful haven with its excellent pebble beach and turquoise ocean, Salcombe, with its green waters and picturesque coves, is a favorite among boaters.

The coast of South Devon is particularly well-known for its picturesque estuaries, like the Teign Estuary and the River Dart, where tourists may go kayaking, boating, or just relaxing and admiring the natural beauty. Charming communities like Totnes, Brixham, and Kingsbridge dot the shoreline here, each providing a unique taste of the seaside.

Best Beaches: From Sandy Shores to Rugged Cliffs

Devon's beaches are as diverse as the surrounding terrain, offering everything from wide sandy beaches that are good for tanning to secluded coves that provide a tranquil haven. These are a few of the county's top beaches.

The North Devon beach of Woolacombe

One of the greatest beaches in the UK is Woolacombe, which is well-known for its three miles of golden sands. Woolacombe provides the ideal balance of coastal enjoyment and scenic beauty, making it ideal for families, surfers, and those seeking to unwind. In addition to its beauty, the beach is regularly ranked as one of the best in the nation for its first-rate amenities and secure swimming areas.

Bantham Beach, located in South Devon

Bantham is a hidden gem in the center of the South Devon Area of Outstanding Natural Beauty. Although surfers enjoy it, the beach is also well-liked for its serene ambiance, which makes it perfect for leisurely stroll down the shore. With Burgh Island rising out of the ocean in the distance, the beach provides breathtaking views of the South Hams.

The North Devon town of Saunton Sands

Saunton Sands is a long, immaculate beach with striking dunes on either side. Saunton Sands is well-liked for surfing, with consistent waves all year round, and is ideal for anyone who like long hikes or a quiet day by the sea. Popular with nature lovers, this beach has breathtaking views of the UNESCO Biosphere Reserve, the Braunton Burrows.

Sands at Blackpool (South Devon)

Blackpool Sands near Dartmouth is a must-see for anyone seeking a more peaceful experience. Blackpool Sands is the ideal location for a restful day by the sea because of its clear water, clean pebble beach, and picturesque setting of rolling hills and pine trees. The beach has great amenities, such as a beach shop and café, and is family-friendly.

The South Devon town of Porthcawl

Porthcawl has everything you could possibly want for a traditional coastal getaway. It is the perfect location for a more exciting beach day because of its wide stretch of sand, exciting activities, and a bustling town with lots of eateries and retail establishments.

Hidden Coves and Secret Spots

There are many undiscovered coves and hideaway locations along Devon's coast where you can get away from the people and take in the peace and quiet. For those who want some privacy while admiring the sea's splendor, these undiscovered treasures are ideal.

Rockham Bay, located in North Devon

Rockham Bay is a remote cove that seems worlds away, nestled on the rim of Morte Point close to Woolacombe. This secret beach, which is reachable via a lovely walk, provides some of the best views in the area along with tranquil tranquility. It is the perfect place for people who want to spend some peaceful time in nature because it is surrounded by cliffs and thick flora.

Smuggler's Cove, located in South Devon

Visit Smuggler's Cove, which is close to Teignmouth, for a genuinely hidden location. One of Devon's most quiet and private places is this little, hidden beach, which is only accessible by foot or boat. Tucked up amongst towering cliffs, it's a wonderful spot to unwind alone and enjoy the breathtaking views.

Beach at Hallsands (South Devon)

One of the county's best-kept secrets is Hallsands Beach, which has a serene and romantic ambience. This serene section of beach, surrounded by striking cliffs and rocky outcrops, is a wonderful getaway from the busier coastal towns.

Coastal Walks: The South West Coast Path

The South West Coast Path is a must-see for anyone wishing to walk Devon's coasts. This famous 630-mile trail travels across Devon's breathtaking coastline from Minehead, Somerset, to Poole Harbour, Dorset.

Hikers may explore Devon's rocky cliffs, remote beaches, and charming communities like Clovelly, Salcombe, and Lynmouth by following the South West Coast Path. The walk is the ideal way to experience the natural beauty of Devon's coast, whether you choose to walk the entire length or just a portion of it.

The South West Coast Path's Highlights

The following are some of Devon's most well-known sections of the South West Coast Path:

Baggy Point: Providing expansive views of Saunton Sands, Croyde Bay, and the rocky coastline beyond.

Dartmouth to Brixham: An wonderful stretch featuring views of the Teign Estuary, woods, and cliffs.

Plymouth to Wembury: This portion offers breathtaking views of the sea and beyond as it passes the iconic Plymouth Hoe.

The South West Coast Path offers countless chances to take in the breathtaking scenery of Devon's coastline, regardless of your level of hiking experience or desire for a leisurely stroll.

Devon's coastlines are a veritable gem, with a variety of sandy beaches, cliffs, and secret locations ideal for adventure and leisure. Devon's coastlines are sure to win your heart and leave you wanting more, whether you're searching for a peaceful day by the sea, a surfing adventure, or a picturesque coastal stroll.

ROLLING COUNTRYSIDE AND NATIONAL PARKS

The countryside of Devon is a tranquil sanctuary where tranquil valleys, undulating hills, and wild moors combine to form an exquisite scenery that appears to have stood the test of time. For nature enthusiasts, hikers, and anybody else wishing to relax in the splendor of the British countryside, Devon's rural districts provide an ideal getaway. These areas include two of the most well-known National Parks in the United Kingdom, Dartmoor and Exmoor, as well as several charming villages and wildlife reserves.

Dartmoor National Park: Wild Beauty and Legends

One of Devon's greatest treasures is Dartmoor National Park, a huge and untamed area that has spawned centuries of tales and legends. An atmosphere of unadulterated beauty can be found in its enigmatic granite tors, old woods, and tussocky moors. Dartmoor, an Area of Outstanding Natural Beauty, is a must-see for anybody traveling to Devon.

A Legendary Landscape

Ancient legends of druidic rituals, spectral wanderers, and phantom hounds that prowl its hills abound in Dartmoor folklore. Authors like Arthur Conan Doyle were influenced by the park's bleak beauty and used it as the setting for his well-known tale, The Hound of the Baskervilles. Nestled at the base of the moors are the quaint settlements of Bovey Tracey and Widecombe-in-the-Moor, each with its own unique customs and stories.

A Sanctuary for Hikers

Dartmoor is a hiker's dream come true for anyone who enjoy being outside. One of the park's most recognizable features are the Tors, which are tall granite formations. Haytor and Sharpitor provide breathtaking views of the surroundings. The South West Coast Path provides easy access to Dartmoor's untamed landscape, where wild ponies wander freely and the air is clear and clean, whether you're planning a quick stroll or a full-day hike.

The park's expansive areas are ideal for a variety of outdoor activities, such as riding horses, cycling, and swimming in its secret streams and pools.

Exmoor National Park: Moorland and Coastal Views

Exmoor National Park, located just north of Dartmoor, is a place that blends breathtaking coastline views with the finest of the British moors. Covering 267 square miles, the park is renowned for its dense forests, high cliffs that drop to the Atlantic Ocean, and rolling moorlands. Exmoor, which combines breathtaking coastline with moorland scenery, provides a whole different experience than Dartmoor.

The Exmoor Hills and Moorlands

The vast and peaceful moorlands of Exmoor give tourists a feeling of isolation and a sense of connectedness to the natural world. One of the park's most well-known locations is the Valley of Rocks, which is close to Lynton. Rugged rock formations border the slopes, creating a spectacular and untamed setting. Herds of wild red deer, one of the park's most recognizable animals, can be found there as well.

The historic breed known as Exmoor Ponies, whose characteristic outlines adorn the wide hillsides of the park, are also found on Exmoor. With birds like the barn owl and peregrine falcon calling Exmoor home, it's a great place for nature lovers to go birdwatching.

Walks by the coast and its beauty

Exmoor's northern coastline is absolutely breathtaking. Exmoor is a stop on the South West Coast Path, where you may stroll along the cliffs and enjoy breath-taking views of the Atlantic Ocean. The combination of rocky moorland and striking coastal landscapes can be explored at the Tale Valley and Lynmouth, where the River Lyn meets the sea. Exmoor is one of the most beautiful national parks in the United Kingdom because of its distinctive blend of sea and moorland.

Picturesque Villages and Rural Escapes

The settlements dotted throughout Devon's undulating hills are a must-see for anybody hoping to capture the essence of the county's most picturesque landscape. These settlements offer an insight of Devonian rural life, complete with thatched homes, country pubs, and local markets.

Clovelly: A Retrospective Look

Many people say that Clovelly, a beautiful seaside community tucked away on North Devon's cliffs, seems to be stuck in a time warp. The settlement can only be reached on foot or by donkey, and the cobbled alleys wind down to the harbor. Because there are no cars in the village, guests can enter a slower, more tranquil world. With its charming cottages, charming beach views, and historic charm, Clovelly offers a memorable rural getaway.

Dunsford and Chagford: Undiscovered Treasures in Dartmoor

The communities of Dunsford and Chagford are tucked away in the heart of Dartmoor National Park. For tourists looking for tranquility in the middle of Dartmoor, these charming little towns are ideal. While Dunsford is tucked away along the banks of the River Teign, encircled by forests and undulating meadows, Chagford offers a variety of traditional tea houses, artisan stores, and local product markets. For those who prefer to take their time discovering Dartmoor's natural splendor, both locations are ideal.

The Villages of South Hams: A Seaside Getaway

The South Hams region, which is located south of Devon, is home to quaint villages like Salcombe, Modbury, and Kingsbridge. These communities provide a laid-back rural lifestyle with the added benefit of being close to beaches. For tourists who want to combine their love of the countryside with convenient access to Devon's breathtaking coasts, these communities are ideal. Salcombe in particular provides a range of water-based sports, such as kayaking and sailing, together with breathtaking views of the Kingsbridge Estuary.

Wildlife and Nature Reserves

Devon is a sanctuary for those who enjoy the outdoors and wildlife because it is home to a wide variety of species and nature reserves. Devon is home to a wide range of animals, including otters, badgers, and an abundance of birds, in addition to its famous red deer and Exmoor ponies.

The Tamar Valley: A Refuge for Wildlife

One of the county's best-kept secrets is the Tamar Valley, which lies on the boundaries of Devon and Cornwall. There are several walking and cycling paths in this Area of Outstanding Natural Beauty, which is also home to a variety of species. Otters and kingfishers can be seen in plenty throughout the valley, particularly around the River Tamar.

The Wildlife Trust of Devon

From its woodlands and moorlands to its wetlands and coastal habitats, the Devon Wildlife Trust strives to protect the county's distinctive environments. The Trust manages a number of nature reserves around Devon, giving tourists plenty of chances to interact with the abundant wildlife of the area.

The vast natural beauty of Devon's undulating landscape allows tourists to explore breathtaking national parks, unwind in quaint villages, and get up close and personal with wildlife and nature reserves. The countryside of Devon is a vital component of the Devon experience, whether you're exploring the ethereal Dartmoor and Exmoor or simply enjoying the tranquility of the county's rural retreats.

HISTORIC SEASIDE TOWNS AND VILLAGES

Devon's coastal towns and villages provide a window into the past, where charming fishing villages, Victorian charm, and Regency grandeur blend with the expansive coastline's natural beauty. Every town has a distinct personality and tale to tell, whether you're taking in the splendor of historic harbors, strolling along seaside promenades, or dining on delicious seafood while taking in the ocean vistas. Let's explore Torquay, Ilfracombe, Sidmouth, and Clovelly—four of Devon's most recognizable coastal treasures.

Torquay: The English Riviera Gem

Torquay, a glitzy beach town that flawlessly combines contemporary conveniences with the elegance of the past, is referred described as the jewel of the English Riviera. Torquay, which lies on Devon's south coast, is well-known for its gorgeous port, pleasant weather, and the fact that Agatha Christie, the Queen of Crime, was born there.

Sunny Shores and Seaside Strolls

Beautiful beaches and palm-lined promenades that create a cozy, friendly ambiance may be found along Torquay's waterfront. The Princess Gardens provide a tranquil area with breathtaking views of the harbor, while Living Coasts, a coastal zoo, lets guests get up close and personal with marine life. Torquay offers something for everyone, whether you want to take a boat excursion, try your hand at water sports, or just unwind by the sea.

Themed Attractions and Victorian Influences

From opulent hotels to sophisticated villas, Torquay's Victorian past is evident in its architectural design. With structures like the Royal Terrace and Torquay Pavilion standing majestically near the seashore, a stroll through the town transports you back in time. The town has a thriving cultural life as well, with a variety of shows held all year round at venues like the Princess Theatre. For anyone looking for a blend of leisure, culture, and history against the breathtaking background of the seaside, Torquay is the perfect destination.

Ilfracombe: Victorian Charm and Dramatic Cliffs

Ilfracombe, a Victorian seaside village farther up the coast, appears to have been designed for people looking for stunning coastal vistas and historic charm. This charming village, tucked up between rocky coasts and tall cliffs, provides an intriguing window into a bygone past.

The Harbor and Famous Points of Interest

The town's main attraction is Ilfracombe's harbor, which is surrounded by striking cliffs. An prominent feature of the town's scenery, the Victorian pier was originally used for passenger ferries. A prime illustration of Ilfracombe's fusion of the modern with the historic, the landmark statue of Verity, a striking modern sculpture by Damien Hirst, sits proudly at the water's edge for visitors who visit the port.

A Legacy of the Victorian Era

With its quaint seaside cottages, terraces, and sophisticated hotels that echo the grandeur of the past, the town's Victorian architecture provides a pleasant trip back in time. Discover the rich history of Ilfracombe by touring the chambers and gardens of Chambercombe Manor, an old manor home that offers a window into the town's past.

Beautiful Beaches and Coastal Walks

Ilfracombe is a great starting point for coastal exploration because of its stunning setting. Explore the South West Coast Path, which offers breathtaking views of the Atlantic Ocean from clifftop walks. Secluded beaches ideal for a tranquil getaway can be reached via the Tunnels Beaches, a distinctive system of tunnels dug through the cliffs. Ilfracombe is a destination worth seeing because of its unique blend of Victorian elegance and coastal beauty.

Sidmouth: Regency Elegance by the Sea

Sidmouth is the ideal location for those looking for a more sedate, sophisticated beach getaway. Sidmouth, which is tucked away in the Jurassic Coast, offers Regency elegance in addition to breathtaking views of the beach and lovely gardens. Sidmouth, renowned for its refined appeal, is a location where leisure, nature, and history all coexist.

The Charm of Regency

Sidmouth's heyday as a chic 19th-century seaside resort is reflected in its Regency architecture, which includes its opulent hotels and terraces. Sidmouth's broad avenues, promenade, and waterfront gardens evoke the relaxed elegance of a bygone period, making a stroll around the town feel like traveling back in time. The town's intriguing past, particularly its ascent as a popular vacation spot during the Regency era, is explored in the Sidmouth Museum.

Seaside strolls and beachside relaxation

Sidmouth boasts a stunning pebble beach that's ideal for lounging in the sun or taking a leisurely dip in the ocean. The town's promenade runs along the shore, providing breathtaking views of the sea and cliffs. Connaught Gardens, which is close by, offers a tranquil haven with its flower-filled walkways and lush foliage. There are several beautiful walks in the East Devon Area of Outstanding Natural Beauty, which is located in the area around Sidmouth, for individuals who enjoy the outdoors.

Clovelly: The Timeless Fishing Village

A charming, car-free fishing village that appears to be frozen in time, Clovelly is one of Devon's most recognizable and classic villages. This hilly village, which is tucked away on the North Devon coast, is well-known for its lovely harbor, whitewashed homes, and cobblestone alleyways.

A Trip Through Time

The community of Clovelly has a peaceful, rustic beauty because cars are not permitted within its boundaries. The village square, where charming houses with flower-filled gardens lie side by side, is reached by a difficult ascent up its winding alleyways from the port. The village is a popular destination for visitors looking for a classic fishing village experience because it is able to preserve its unspoiled nature due to the lack of cars.

The Seaside Beauty and the Harbor

The center of Clovelly is the port. Visitors can observe local fisherman bringing in their daily catch as traditional fishing boats depart from this location. Cliffs encircle the port, and the gorgeous surroundings make it the perfect place for a leisurely walk or a boat excursion. Views of the surrounding countryside and the charm of the village may be found in Clovelly Court Gardens.

The Ideal Getaway

For people looking for a classic getaway from the stress of contemporary life, Clovelly is the ideal location. Its charming port and serene, picturesque streets provide a window into Devon's traditional coastal way of life. Visitors are welcome to unwind and take in the allure of a community that hasn't altered much in decades.

Devon boasts some of the most stunning and enchanting beach towns and villages in the United Kingdom. Every town has something wonderful and distinctive to offer every tourist, from the timeless charm of Clovelly to the glitz of Torquay. Devon's coast is teeming with hidden gems just waiting to be discovered, whether you're searching for Victorian grandeur, Regency grace, or the classic charm of a fishing community.

FOOD AND DRINK IN DEVON

In Devon, eating is an experience rather than merely a meal. The county's culinary offerings, which range from the freshest seafood to the richest cream teas, are rooted in tradition yet constantly changing to reflect contemporary trends. Devon's culinary scene will leave you wanting more, whether you're dining at a classy restaurant, a charming café, or a rustic pub. Let's explore Devon's flavors, where every morsel reveals a tale of the land and sea.

Devonshire Cream Tea: Where to Find the Best

Enjoying Devonshire cream tea, the county's specialty, is a must-do while visiting Devon. But let's correct the record before we explore the top locations to savor this classic treat. In Devon, scones, clotted cream, and jam are the main ingredients. In typical Devonian fashion, the cream is added first, then the jam. The sequence is the opposite in nearby Cornwall, so it's a scone showdown. Regardless, it's a taste of heritage and history, and Devon is the ideal location to savor it.

How to Locate the Greatest Cream Teas

There are many tearooms and cafés in Devon that provide delicious cream teas, but some of the greatest places are Bayard's Cove Café in Dartmouth, where you can eat a scone while taking in the beauty of the harbor. Another local favourite is the Cream Tea Café in Sidmouth, which serves freshly made scones with clotted cream that almost melts in your mouth. The Devonshire Tea Rooms in Tavistock provide the ideal location for enjoying this traditional treat in a cozy and pleasant environment for a more private, rural experience.

Fresh Seafood and Local Delicacies

Devon, being a coastal county, is well known for its fresh seafood that is taken off its coast Because of its closeness to the Atlantic Ocean and the English Channel, the area is a great place to enjoy some of the best fish and shellfish the UK has to offer. Regardless matter your preference for crab, lobster, or the classic fish and chips, Devon's seafood will captivate you.

Seafood You Must Try

Brixham is the place to go if you want fresh fish. Some of the best seafood restaurants in the area may be found in Brixham, which is well-known for its busy waterfront. At eateries like The Crab Shack, which is located directly on the water, you can try the renowned Brixham crab, fish chowder, and pan-fried scallops. As an alternative, Salcombe, with its charming harbor, is home to several seafood eateries that serve the day's fish while taking in breathtaking views.

Additionally, don't pass up trying Devon's mussels. Usually served with garlic and cream, these luscious, plump mussels provide a sumptuous touch to any meal. Naturally, Devon's traditional fish and chips—crispy batter, flakey fish, and flawlessly golden fries—are the best.

Best Pubs and Fine Dining Experiences

In addition to having great seafood, Devon is home to a wide range of pubs and restaurants that provide a more extensive selection of regional specialties and fine dining experiences. Devon has everything you need, whether you're craving a quick snack or an unforgettable gourmet dining experience.

Character-Driven Pubs

Hearty meals and refreshing local ales are provided in Devon's many classic rural taverns. In a quaint, rustic setting, the Merrymoor Inn in Crackington Haven, close to the North Devon shore, serves roast dinners, delicious steak pies, and regional beers. The Royal Oak in Dartmoor, which has been feeding both locals and tourists for generations, offers a vibrant environment together with a little piece of local history. Classic roast lamb, beef wellington, and other hearty treats are on its locally sourced menu.

The Galleon Inn in Teignmouth provides a blend of regional cuisine with a modern twist for those looking for a more contemporary take on pub fare. This lively location, which offers breathtaking views of the port, combines the finest traditional Devon dishes with a chic, contemporary atmosphere.

Elegant Dining with a Regional Influence

Devon is home to several Michelin-starred restaurants and fine dining experiences that emphasize regional and seasonal produce if you're in the mood for something more upscale. Torquay's Elephant Restaurant has a modern menu that combines inventive cooking methods with locally sourced, fresh ingredients. Every meal showcases Devon's amazing variety of food and is a work of art.

The Jack in the Green in Rockbeare is another great option for a fine dining experience in the middle of the countryside. It's ideal for anyone who want to savor a wonderful meal with a local twist because of its warm, sophisticated ambiance and menu that highlights regional Devon meats and veggies.

Wineries, Breweries, and Cider Farms

Without acknowledging Devon's flourishing wineries, breweries, and cider farms, its culinary scene would be incomplete. There are several great drinks to go with your meal, ranging from award-winning wines to craft ales and traditional Devon ciders.

Wines from Devon

One of the UK's undiscovered treasures is the wine country of Devon. Many of the very exceptional wines produced by the county's vineyards have taken home national honors. Award-winning wine tastings and guided vineyard tours are available at Sharpham Vineyard, which is close to Totnes. West Devon's Rixcote Vineyard has an amazing selection of English sparkling wines that are ideal for celebrating special events if you're looking for something a little more unusual.

Devon Cider and Craft Breweries

A visit to Devon wouldn't be complete without indulging in a cool pint of local beer or a cider produced using apples grown in the area. Devon has a long history of producing cider, and locations such as Sandford Orchards provide wonderful selections of both classic and creative ciders. In the meanwhile, Otter Brewery and Devon Brew Co. provide an amazing assortment of craft ales, crafted with love and care, ranging from classic bitters to experimental IPAs.

Devon offers foodies a gastronomic journey, from the classic treats of Devonshire cream tea to the freshest fish and an abundance of regional beverages. The region's outstanding pubs, fine dining establishments, and wineries, along with the local specialties, make it a trip that foodies will love. Your taste buds are in for a treat in Devon, whether you're enjoying a glass of local wine, a leisurely cream tea, or the day's catch.

OUTDOOR ADVENTURES AND ACTIVITIES

Devon is a paradise for adventure seekers, with its breathtaking natural surroundings beckoning you to explore and test your mettle in a variety of outdoor pursuits. Devon has something to offer everyone, whether you're drawn to the coast for unusual wildlife encounters, the countryside for a tranquil getaway, or the water for an exhilarating experience. Devon's outdoor experiences guarantee an amazing journey, from horseback riding in rolling hills, trekking through picturesque national parks, surfing on the rocky beaches, and even seeing dolphins off the coast.

Water Sports: Surfing, Kayaking, and Paddleboarding

For those looking for an energetic water adventure, Devon's coastline is the perfect playground. It provides some of the greatest surfing, kayaking, and paddleboarding experiences in the UK because of its stunning beaches and striking cliffs.

Devon Surfing: Seize the Wave

Devon is renowned for having great surf conditions, particularly in the North Devon area, which has a variety of beaches ideal for waves. With their long, sandy beaches and reliable waves, Croyde Bay and Saunton Sands are two of the most well-liked locations for surfers. These beaches offer ideal conditions for surfers of all skill levels, as well as surf schools that can teach you how to ride the waves.

Try Woolacombe Beach or Putsborough Sands for a more casual surfing experience. Both provide great surf conditions and calmer waters for a more laid-back atmosphere. Devon's surf schools make it simple for anyone to get on a board and ride the waves, regardless of experience level.

Paddleboarding and Kayaking: serene waters and picturesque vistas

Kayaking and paddleboarding are a thrilling way to explore Devon's coastlines, rivers, and secret coves if you're looking for a different kind of water experience. Because it's simpler to learn and provides fantastic views of the ocean and surroundings, paddleboarding is a favorite family pastime. Two excellent paddleboarding spots with serene waters and breathtaking scenery are Salcombe and Dartmouth. On a board or kayak, you may explore the Salcombe Estuary, where the crystal-clear water reveals secret beaches, verdant vegetation, and intriguing fauna.

River kayaking, which offers a tranquil, quiet opportunity to enjoy nature while paddling along the water's edge, is a terrific option for people seeking a more strenuous experience in areas like the Tamar Valley. You will enjoy the pristine beauty of the region as you fly by fields, forests, and old bridges.

Hiking and Cycling Trails

Devon is a hiker's and cyclist's dream come true because of its diverse scenery, which includes everything from spectacular cliffs and rocky beaches to undulating hills and historic woodlands. There is a trail for every level of adventurer, whether you're searching for a leisurely walk by the shore or a more strenuous hike through the countryside.

Devon Hiking: Beautiful Paths and Stunning Views

With miles of trails that go through untamed moorlands, old woodlands, and charming valleys, Dartmoor National Park and Exmoor National Park are two of the county's most well-liked hiking locations. Visit Haytor, a granite hill in Dartmoor, for a short, family-friendly hike. From the summit, you can take in breath-taking views of the surrounding moors.

The South West Coast Path is one of the most beautiful and fulfilling long-distance hikes in the UK if you're searching for something more strenuous. This trail, which covers more than 600 miles, leads you along the Devon coastline's striking cliffs, secluded coves, and golden beaches. You will be rewarded with breathtaking views of the Atlantic Ocean, seabirds, and verdant farmland whether you choose to walk a few miles or the full distance.

Hike to Hound Tor on Dartmoor for a more historical viewpoint. There, you may discover prehistoric monuments and ancient stone circles, giving your outdoor trip a cultural touch.

Cycling in Devon: Explore the Rural Landscape

Some of the UK's greatest cycling routes may be found in Devon. There are many opportunities to explore the county's many landscapes thanks to its designated bike trails, quiet country lanes, and seaside routes. One of the most well-liked cycling routes in the area is the 180-mile Tarka Trail, which winds across North Devon and offers stunning scenery, serene rivers, and serene rural areas while you bike.

The South Devon Coastal Path provides a cycling challenge with expansive views of the sea and rocky cliffs if you'd rather take a more coastal path. Enjoying Devon's breathtaking beauty on two wheels is made simple by the diversity of cycling routes, whether you're riding slowly through the picturesque villages or taking on the hills and valleys.

Horseback Riding in the Countryside

One of the greatest locations in the UK for equestrian riding is Devon. Few other sports may help you connect with nature like horseback riding, with its expansive expanses of open moorland, stunning countryside, and ocean views. Horseback riding provides an unmatched chance to experience the county's natural splendor from a different angle.

Riding in Exmoor and Dartmoor

Excellent equestrian riding is one of Dartmoor National Park's most well-known features. You may ride for hours through the park's famous granite tors and old-growth forests on its miles of open moorland and rural bridleways. Trek through Exmoor for a more difficult journey. Exmoor, which is well-known for its untamed ponies and expansive hills, has a variety of guided horseback riding trips that will transport you through the center of this untamed and breathtaking national park.

From leisurely trots through picturesque villages to more daring excursions across the moors and coastal trails, Devon is home to numerous riding schools and stables that provide guided rides. Regardless of your level of skill, horseback riding in Devon will allow you to fully appreciate the natural beauty of the county.

Wildlife Watching: Seals, Dolphins, and Birds

Devon is a great spot to observe animals because of its abundant natural sceneries. You'll have the opportunity to see a variety of amazing species in their native environments whether you're trekking through the countryside, out on the lake, or just admiring the scenery.

Finding Dolphins and Seals

Seals and dolphins are two of the most recognizable animals along the coast. Visit Lundy Island, a nature reserve, where you may see harbor seals and Atlantic grey seals swimming in the waves or lounging on the rocks. Both bottlenose and common dolphins are regularly sighted off the coast of Dartmouth, making it another popular destination for dolphin sightings. Consider going on a whale-watching excursion for a unique experience, where you might also see porpoises, whales, and a variety of seabirds.

Observing birds in the Nature Reserves in Devon

Some of the UK's top locations for birding may be found in Devon. Many different types of birds have great habitats in the Tamar Valley, Exmoor, and Dartmoor. In the area's nature reserves, twitchers will love the opportunity to see barn owls, red grouse, and peregrine falcons. Devon is a top destination for environment lovers and wildlife enthusiasts because of its diverse landscapes, which serve as a home for a variety of bird species.

Devon provides an amazing array of outdoor experiences, like trekking across old moors, surfing the waves, horseback riding through picturesque landscapes, and observing seals playing in the water. Devon's expansive outdoors guarantee that you'll never run out of things to enjoy, whether your goal is an adrenaline rush or just to get in touch with nature.

DEVON FOR FAMILIES

For families seeking a combination of outdoor experiences, educational opportunities, and enjoyable activities, Devon is a fantastic destination. Every family member, from young children to elderly parents, will have a great time in Devon thanks to its breathtaking natural beauty, charming communities, and an abundance of attractions suitable for all ages. Devon's family-friendly atmosphere is likely to make an impression, whether you're touring interactive museums, creating sandcastles on the beach, or having an animal encounter.

Top Family-Friendly Attractions

There are several family-friendly sites in Devon that provide entertainment and educational possibilities. Devon has much to pique your children's interest, whether they are history aficionados or nature lovers.

The RAMM, or Royal Albert Memorial Museum

A great place for a family adventure is the Royal Albert Memorial Museum (RAMM), which is situated in the center of Exeter. From dinosaur fossils and ancient Egyptian mummies to international cultures and artwork, RAMM's diverse exhibitions make learning fun and interesting for kids. Children may explore the exhibits through interactive activities like drawing, crafts, or even dressing up as historical individuals thanks to the museum's frequent special family events and workshops.

Farm at Pennywell

Children and families may have an exciting day at Pennywell Farm in South Devon if they want a more immersive animal experience. Children can interact with a range of animals at this functioning farm, including goats, ducks, pigs, and horses. There are lots of play areas and tractor rides to keep kids occupied, and they can try feeding and touching the animals. Pennywell is a popular destination for animal lovers because it also provides a "piggy cuddles" session for smaller kids.

The Sanctuary for Donkeys

Another great family-friendly destination is the Donkey Sanctuary at Sidmouth, a bit further south. Families can take guided tours, meet and learn about the sanctuary's rescued donkeys, and even adopt a donkey for the day here. The sanctuary offers a free admission experience that encourages compassion and respect for animals, making it ideal for low-income families.

Beaches with Safe Swimming Areas

Families who enjoy the sea will love Devon's beaches. From young children swimming in the shallows to older children learning to surf, there is a beach for every member of the family along the kilometers of coastline that offer protected coves, smooth sand, and quiet waves.

Woolacombe Beach

One of the most well-liked family beaches in the UK is Woolacombe Beach in North Devon. With more than three miles of golden beaches, children have plenty of room to run, play, and construct sandcastles. Because lifeguards are on duty during the summer, the waters are safe for swimming. Families may easily spend the entire day by the sea thanks to the beach's excellent amenities, which include eateries and picnic spots. You may even expose the kids to the pleasures of surfing by renting a bodyboard or surfboard for a little extra enjoyment.

Sands in Blackpool

Another great beach choice for families with little children is Blackpool Sands, which is close to Dartmouth. The surrounding pine trees provide a picturesque backdrop, while the water is serene, clean, and ideal for safe swimming. Families can try their hand at water sports together by using the designated kayaking and paddleboarding area. After spending some time in the sun, unwind at the neighborhood café, which serves delectable cuisine and beverages for a revitalizing respite.

Bigbury-on-Sea

Another fantastic family vacation spot is Bigbury-on-Sea in South Devon. Its shallow waters make it safe for younger children, and its sandy beach is perfect for swimming. The famous Art Deco hotel on Burgh Island gives your trip a mystical touch. Along the shoreline, there are additional rock pools where kids can explore and look for little fish, crabs, and shells.

Adventure Parks and Zoos

Devon offers a variety of adventure parks and zoos with thrilling displays and activities for families looking for more active thrills and the opportunity to get up close and personal with exotic creatures.

Theme Park & Resort Crealy

Crealy Theme Park & Resort, which is close to Exeter, is one of Devon's best family attractions. Families with kids of all ages will love this day trip, which is full of thrilling rides, adventure play zones, and live performances. There is something for everyone in the park thanks to its themed rides, which include water slides and roller coasters. For smaller kids, there's a soft play area, a bouncy castle, and zip lines at the adventure park. The resort on-site allows you to remain longer, which makes it ideal for a prolonged family vacation.

Zoo in Paignton

The Paignton Zoo is a must-see for those who enjoy animals. With more than 2,000 animals, such as lions, giraffes, and meerkats, it offers kids both entertainment and knowledge. With so many open areas to run and explore, Paignton Zoo's beautiful grounds make the ideal backdrop for a family outing. In order to ensure that children learn while having fun, the zoo also conducts participatory events like animal feedings and speeches.

Adventure Wonderland

Adventure Wonderland in Exmouth is a delightful family park with rides, playgrounds, and attractions modeled by Alice in Wonderland that is ideal for younger kids. Younger children will love the mild rides, such as the maze, a pirate ship, and the teacup ride. Children can let their imaginations run free in this quirky environment.

Rainy Day Activities for Kids

Even while Devon's bright days are ideal for outdoor recreation, families can find plenty to do indoors when it starts to rain. Rain or shine, your family can still enjoy an entertaining day thanks to these attractions.

The Underground Passages of Exeter

The Exeter Underground Passages are a system of ancient tunnels beneath the city that offer an educational experience with a dash of adventure. Children may explore the chilly, evocative tunnels and learn about Exeter's history by taking a guided tour. It offers an intriguing blend of entertainment and instruction, making it a distinctive way to spend a few hours.

Model Village of Babbacombe

Babbacombe Model Village near Torquay is a great family destination, rain or shine. Set amid exquisitely planted gardens, this award-winning attraction showcases painstakingly crafted miniature landscapes, buildings, and even trains. The children may explore the small world, which is full with humorous details, for hours on end. With its interactive exhibits and indoor displays, it's the ideal place to go on wet days.

The Allotment for Children

Situated in the charming town of Topsham, the Children's Allotment offers young families an interactive and instructive experience. Children can sow seeds, learn about the natural world, and even take home their own little plants in this covered area, even in inclement weather.

With a wide variety of activities suitable for all ages, Devon is the ideal vacation spot for families. Your family will never run out of things to see and do, from rainy-day diversions to adventure parks, family-friendly sites, and beaches with safe swimming. Devon makes sure there's something for everyone to enjoy, whether you're looking for thrills at a theme park, discovering wildlife, or splashing in the water. So prepare for an exciting family trip in one of the most stunning regions of the United Kingdom by packing your bags!

ROMANTIC DEVON

Devon's stunning coastlines, undulating countryside, and quaint villages make it a romantic location for couples. Devon has a wealth of chances to make treasured moments with your significant other, whether you're searching for a quiet hideaway, a picnic at sunset, or a restorative spa treatment. Allow this charming county's natural splendor to create the ideal setting for romance.

Private Retreats and Comfortable Hotels

There is nothing more romantic than retreating to a little hideaway where you and your significant other can relax in a quiet, private environment. Devon offers a range of upscale cottages, boutique inns, and rural hideaways that make the ideal setting for a romantic vacation.

Park Gidleigh, Dartmoor

Gidleigh Park on Dartmoor provides a private country home experience with exquisite dining, tasteful rooms, and breathtaking views of the surrounding moorland for a decadent getaway.

Long walks on private trails, lounging by the fire in the lounge, or indulging in a fine supper at the hotel's acclaimed restaurant are all options for couples.

Babbacombe's Cary Arms & Spa

Luxurious rooms and private beach huts with an ocean view are available at the cozy seaside getaway The Cary Arms & Spa, which is tucked away on the coast. Sip champagne on your private patio, relax with a couples massage at the spa, and wake up to the sound of the waves. This is the perfect romantic getaway because of its luxurious comforts and stunning coastline.

Manor Lewtrenchard, West Devon

With its antique-filled chambers, lovely gardens, and candlelit dinners, Lewtrenchard Manor, a historic country estate, evokes old-world romanticism in a setting reminiscent of a fairy tale. It's ideal for couples that appreciate classic charm and history.

Locations for Sunsets and Beautiful Picnic Areas

Watching a sunset with your significant other is one of the most romantic activities you can do, and Devon offers some of the most beautiful locations for this activity. Bring a blanket, pack a picnic, and allow the golden tones of the waning sun to create a momentous occasion.

South Devon's Burgh Island

Accessible by a special marine tractor, Burgh Island is a picturesque location for a picnic at twilight. It's a memorable spot to watch the sun set because of its breathtaking coastal scenery and fascinating history.

Exmoor's Valley of Rocks

Exmoor's Valley of Rocks provides a rocky yet breathtaking backdrop for couples who enjoy a little drama. The views are breathtaking from this high-altitude location, and the sunset over the Atlantic makes for a memorable sight.

The beach at Bigbury on Sea

Bigbury-on-Sea Beach is ideal if you like a traditional coastal romance. Have a picnic on the sand or take a leisurely walk along the water's edge as the sun sets over the softly crashing waves.

Romantic Coastal Walks

Walking hand in hand along a picturesque beach path is one of Devon's most straightforward yet romantic experiences. Some of England's most exquisite and private walking pathways may be found along the South West Coast Path, which runs the length of the county.

Hope Cove to Salcombe

There are many private places to stop and enjoy the scenery along this remote coastal trail, which passes through charming villages, golden beaches, and sheer cliffs. It's the ideal walk for couples looking for peace and quiet because of the peaceful coves along the route, which are perfect for a romantic rest.

The Cobbled Streets of Clovelly

Discover the quaint, car-free village of Clovelly, with its picturesque harbor, whitewashed houses, and winding cobbled streets, and travel back in time. The town is a very romantic destination to stroll with your significant other because of its historic beauty and sea vistas.

Railway Walk at Lynton & Lynmouth Cliff

Consider the ancient funicular railway, the Lynton & Lynmouth Cliff Railway, which provides breathtaking panoramic views, for something a little different. After reaching the summit, take in the sea breeze while strolling along the coastline route before stopping at a charming café for afternoon tea.

Spa Retreats and Luxury Escapes

Devon's spa getaways provide the ideal balance of luxury and closeness for couples wishing to let their hair down and truly relax together. These opulent spas, which feature hot tubs with views of the beach and wellness experiences in the countryside, create the ideal setting for a romantic getaway.

Dartmoor's Bovey Castle Spa

Bovey Castle is a five-star getaway with luxurious spa services, an indoor pool, and breathtaking views, all set in the undulating hills of Dartmoor. End the day with a private meal in the castle's exquisite restaurant, unwind in the sauna, and get a massage next to each other.

Sands Hotel & Spa in Saunton

The Saunton Sands Hotel & Spa, which overlooks North Devon's beautiful beaches, is the perfect place for couples who enjoy wellness activities and the sea. The opulent spa has a thermal suite, a heated outdoor pool, and an oceanfront hot tub that's ideal for sipping champagne while watching the waves.

In Mawgan Porth, the Scarlet Hotel

The Scarlet Hotel has a lighted relaxation area, Ayurvedic spa treatments, and a clifftop hot tub for an eco-luxury spa experience. This boutique hotel, which is just for adults, is a quiet haven where couples may relax in elegance.

Devon is a romantic paradise, with its private retreats, breathtaking walks along the coast, and little spas that provide for the ideal backdrop for special occasions. Devon offers a plethora of chances to spend time with your significant other in an amazing environment, whether you're strolling through quaint seaside towns, enjoying opulent spa treatments, or watching the sunset from a secluded cove.

Devon offers romance, leisure, and breathtaking scenery at every turn, whether you're organizing a honeymoon, anniversary, or just a memorable vacation. Thus, take a vacation to this charming area and use the moors, waves, and sunsets to inspire your own romantic tale.

ARTS, CULTURE, AND LOCAL TRADITIONS

Devon's landscapes, villages, and people are intricately linked with its rich artistic and cultural legacy. Devon is a place where creativity and heritage coexist, from its literary ties and thriving theater industry to its traditional crafts and folk festivals. Devon's culture is just as fascinating as its landscape, whether you're visiting the homes of well-known authors, going to a vibrant music festival, or perusing artisan markets.

Devon's Literary and Artistic Heritage

Devon's spectacular beaches, untamed moors, and charming villages have long served as a source of inspiration for authors, poets, and artists.

The English Riviera and Agatha Christie

The well-known "Queen of Crime," Agatha Christie, is among Devon's most well-known authors. She was born in Torquay but lived in Devon for a large portion of her life, and the landscapes of Devon are reflected in several of her writings. Fans may see her gorgeous vacation home on the River Dart, Greenway House, which is now a National Trust property and contains many of her personal belongings. Torquay honors her legacy each September with the International Agatha Christie Festival, which includes interactive murder mystery events, plays, and speeches.

Dartmoor and Sir Arthur Conan Doyle

Fans of Sherlock Holmes, who were influenced by Doyle's time in Devon, may recognize the spooky beauty of Dartmoor from The Hound of the Baskervilles. The lonesome moorland pathways, old ruins, and mist-covered tors make it the ideal backdrop for gothic intrigue. Fans of literature can visit Baskerville Hall, Hound Tor, and Grimspound, which are all rumored to have served as inspiration for his well-known book.

Devon landscapes and artists

For ages, Devon's undulating hills, rocky cliffs, and serene harbors have also drawn painters and photographers. The area boasts a flourishing art culture, especially in Dartmouth and St Ives (just across the Cornish border), where galleries display regional paintings of the landscape and seascapes. Art enthusiasts can participate in Totnes Art & Design Festival, which honors Devon's creative energy, or visit Thelma Hulbert Gallery in Honiton, which hosts modern exhibitions.

Music and Theatre Scene

Devon has a thriving performing arts culture that includes both contemporary music facilities and historic playhouses. There is something for every cultural aficionado, whether they enjoy folk performances in a welcoming tavern, classical music, or modern theater.

Royal Plymouth Theatre

The Theatre Royal Plymouth, the biggest and most prominent theater in the South West, presents original shows, traveling plays, and West End productions. For theatergoers seeking top-notch comedies, musicals, and dramas, it's a must-see.

The Northcott Theatre in Exeter

The Exeter Northcott Theatre, which frequently draws inspiration from Devon's history and culture, presents classical plays, experimental performances, and local productions for a more personal experience.

Venues for Folk and Live Music

Devon boasts a flourishing folk music culture, with both traditional and modern folk musicians performing in local pubs, festivals, and concert venues. Among the top locations are:

The Barrel House in Totnes is a warm and inviting space that hosts acoustic, jazz, and folk performances.

Torrington's Plough Arts Centre is a community-driven venue for live theater, movies, and music.

Plymouth's unique B-Bar features live jazz, world, and blues music performances.

A local tavern's shanty night (sea shanty singing) is a must-attend for anyone wishing to become fully immersed in Devon's folk customs!

Folk Festivals and Local Celebrations

Devon's festivals offer an intriguing look into local life with their lively blend of storytelling, dance, music, and customs.

The Sidmouth Folk Festival

The Sidmouth Folk Festival, one of the most renowned folk music and dance festivals in the UK, together storytellers, dancers, and musicians from all over the nation. A vibrant and engaging atmosphere is created by the week-long event's concerts, ceilidhs (group dances), craft booths, and street acts.

The Widecombe Fair

This centuries-old fair honors Devon's rural customs and is held in the quaint village of Widecombe-in-the-Moor on Dartmoor. Horse-drawn cart rides, cattle displays, traditional music, and the fair's well-known folk song, "Uncle Tom Cobley," are all available to visitors.

The Royal Regatta of Dartmouth

The Dartmouth Royal Regatta, a staple of Devon's summer schedule, combines athletic competitions, maritime traditions, and exciting entertainment. There will be a lot of music, dancing, and carnival festivities, along with boat races and fireworks.

In Ottery St. Mary, Pixie Day

Pixie Day in Ottery St Mary is a lighthearted homage to the many pixie and spirit myths found in Devon mythology. The festival, which is held every June, is a joyful and mischievous parade in which children dressed as pixies take over the town and reenact the local legend of the pixies being expelled from the church.

Traditional Crafts and Markets

Beyond music and painting, Devon's artistic legacy includes artisan markets and craftsmanship, where old skills are preserved.

Ceramics and Pottery

For locally produced ceramics, woodworking, and textiles, Bovey Tracey's Devon Guild of Craftsmen is a must-see.

The Honiton Pottery Honiton, renowned for its exquisite hand-painted ceramics, is a wonderful destination for touring pottery studios and purchasing one-of-a-kind mementos.

Handmade Wool Crafts and Textiles

Wool production has a long history in Devon, going all the way back to the Middle Ages. In communities like Ashburton and Totnes, wool crafts and handweaving are still performed today, and tourists can buy locally produced sweaters, blankets, and scarves.

Food artisans and farmers' markets

Visit the nearby farmers' markets for a genuine flavor of Devonian workmanship. There, you can discover:

- Handcrafted chutneys and cheeses
- Conventional mead and cider
- Devonshire honey with freshly made scones

Notable markets that provide a lively blend of regional products, crafts, and street acts are the Totnes Good Food Market and the Exeter Farmers' Market.

Devon's rich history and inventive spirit are reflected in its arts, culture, and customs. Every encounter is filled with a feeling of location and history, whether you're exploring artisan markets, going to a vibrant folk festival, or entering the world of Agatha Christie.

Devon has a vibrant and immersive cultural landscape that will enthrall history buffs, art aficionados, and inquisitive tourists alike, from musical village fairs to theatrical productions in opulent playhouses. Devon's artistic character and regional customs guarantee that every visit is full of creativity, inspiration, and life-changing experiences, regardless of your interest.

ANNUAL EVENTS AND FESTIVALS IN 2025

Devon's calendar is jam-packed with exciting festivals and events that honor everything from regional cuisine and beverages to history, music, and outdoor pursuits. 2025 offers an interesting schedule of events, whether your interests are in world-class seafood, folk music by the sea, or historical reenactments.

This is a list of must-see activities that will add even more special memories to your trip to Devon.

Food and Drink Festivals
October 2025: Dartmouth Food Festival

Foodies should not miss the Dartmouth Food Festival, one of the best food festivals in the UK. This event, which takes place in the picturesque seaside town of Dartmouth, brings together food enthusiasts, artisan producers, and famous chefs for a weekend of workshops, tastings, and cooking demos. You may anticipate tasting Devon's renowned cream teas, locally produced ciders, artisan cheeses, and fresh seafood.

Highlights:

- Live cooking demonstrations by chefs with Michelin stars
- Devon's finest suppliers at a busy food market
- Tastings of wines and gins with knowledgeable sommeliers

FoodFest in North Devon (September 2025)

The North Devon FoodFest, which celebrates the region's varied culinary scene, is held in Barnstaple. This event highlights the best of sustainable and local cuisine, from contemporary fusion meals to traditional Devonshire pasties.

Highlights:

- Fresh seafood from street food vendors
- Workshops on cooking that are suitable for families
- Samples of craft beer and cider from nearby breweries

Devon County Show (Westpoint Arena, Exeter, May 2025)

One of the county's largest yearly events, the Devon County Show combines entertainment, farming, and food. Savor locally grown vegetables that has won awards, observe livestock contests, and have a fun-filled day with the family.

Don't overlook:

Devon's Finest Food and Drink Pavilion

Equestrian competitions and sheepdog trials

The record-breaking Devonshire custom of the enormous cream tea gathering!

Music and Cultural Events
2025's Sidmouth Folk Festival, August 2–9.

This seaside village becomes a cultural center during the Sidmouth Folk Festival, a week-long festival of folk music, dance, and storytelling. A vibrant blend of street acts, sea shanties, ceilidhs (traditional dances), and concerts can be anticipated.

Highlights of the Festival:

- Live performances by well-known folk performers
- Participatory dance classes that teach you how to do traditional Morris dance!
- Family storytelling sessions by the sea

Beautiful Days Festival (Escot Park, close to Exeter, August 2025)

Beautiful Days is Devon's version of Glastonbury, a free music festival with a relaxed vibe. The festival features a diverse lineup of rock, indie, folk, and world music groups and is situated in a charming park.

Anticipate:

- A designated children's area and a family-friendly atmosphere
- A thriving festival food village and craft market
- A spectacular fireworks show to wrap up the occasion

Festival of the Two Moors (October 2025, Multiple Locations)

The Two Moors Festival is a must-attend event for fans of classical music. This event, which spans Dartmoor and Exmoor, features performances by top musicians in small settings, country homes, and historic churches.

Historic Reenactments and Folk Traditions

Widecombe Fair (Dartmoor, September 2025)

Widecombe Fair is an iconic Devonian tradition that dates back generations. The fair, which has its roots in agricultural and rural customs, includes traditional music, livestock displays, and horse-drawn carts.

Events you must attend:

A well-known folk ballad served as the inspiration for the fabled Uncle Tom Cobley march.

Sheepdog performances featuring expert farm dogs

Devon's historical breeds are highlighted in the traditional Dartmoor pony show.

May 3–5, 2025: Brixham Pirate Festival

Mateys, aha! One of the most exciting pirate-themed events in the UK, the Brixham Pirate Festival attracts fans from all across the nation. With live reenactments, sea shanties, and cannon fire, the historic fishing village of Brixham turns into a sanctuary for buccaneers, smugglers, and pirates.

Pirate fun consists of:

- Battles and skirmishes in real time in the harbor
- Dress up as your favorite pirate for a costume parade!
- Family-friendly events such as storytelling and treasure hunts

The June 2025 Powderham Castle Medieval Festival will take place close to Exeter.

Visit Powderham Castle to travel back in time, as lords, knights, and jesters bring the past to life. This medieval celebration includes dining banquets, falconry performances, and jousting competitions.

Highlights:

- Demos of sword fighting and live-action knight battles
- Classical medieval dance and music
- A medieval costume and handcrafted crafts bazaar in a castle

Adventure and Outdoor Festivals
OceanFest (Croyde Bay, June 2025)

OceanFest is North Devon's premier beach festival, combining surfing, music, and sustainability in a unique way. This event draws surfers, athletes, and ocean enthusiasts because of the ideal backdrop provided by the waves of Croyde Bay.

Highlights of the festival:

- Surfing contests with the best surfers in the UK
- Sessions of coasteering, paddleboarding, and beach yoga
- A lively, summertime-themed live music lineup

English Riviera Airshow (Torbay, May 2025)

The English Riviera Airshow provides a breathtaking show of military aircraft, antique aircraft, and aerobatic maneuvers over the breathtaking Torbay coastline for aviation lovers.

A must-see

- Amazing flying feats performed by the Red Arrows
- Lancaster bombers and historic Spitfires in flight
- A vintage automobile show and a family funfair

Dartmoor Walking Festival (Dartmoor National Park, August 2025)

Local historians, rangers, and outdoor experts lead guided walks around Dartmoor as part of this event, which celebrates hiking, heritage, and ecology.

Highlights:

- Moorland hiking with a guide, ranging from leisurely walks to strenuous hikes
- Narrative walks examining the tales and legends of Dartmoor
- Expeditions to observe wildlife, such as birding and wild pony trails

In 2025, Devon has a lot to offer tourists with its many festivals and cultural events. Devon's festivals bring the county's rich history and scenic beauty to life, whether you're savoring regional food, taking in live music, exploring history, or enjoying the great outdoors.

There will undoubtedly be an event that catches your attention whenever you visit, so make sure to write the date on your calendar, gather your belongings, and get ready to enjoy Devon's finest!

DEVON'S ECO-FRIENDLY & SUSTAINABLE TRAVEL

Devon's stunning scenery, which includes rocky coasts and undulating moorlands, is a priceless asset that should be preserved. Adopting sustainable travel practices can help protect this breathtaking area for future generations, whether you're enjoying the verdant countryside, the golden beaches of South Devon, or the huge wilderness of Dartmoor.

Reducing your effect is only one aspect of sustainable tourism in Devon; other aspects include getting fully immersed in the local way of life, helping out small businesses, and taking in genuine experiences that honor the area's customs and natural beauty.

Green Accommodations and Eco-Lodges

One of the best ways to make your trip to Devon more sustainable is to book eco-friendly lodging. Throughout the county, a large number of hotels, guesthouses, and resorts are dedicated to eco-friendly operations such waste minimization, water conservation, and renewable energy.

Devon's Best Eco-Friendly Places to Stay

The Old Rectory Hotel (Exmoor National Park) is a quaint, solar-powered boutique hotel with a dedication to wildlife conservation and organic food that is sourced locally.

Ladram Bay Vacation Park on the Jurassic Coast This family-friendly beachfront getaway, which is a prime example of sustainable tourism, offers eco-friendly activities, EV charging stations, and solar-powered amenities.

Dartmoor Shepherds Huts: With wood-burning stoves and composting toilets, these off-grid huts offer a comfortable, low-impact stay in the center of Dartmoor for glamping enthusiasts.

You can sleep amid the trees at the Bulworthy Project (North Devon), a forest eco-lodge that promotes conservation and reforestation.

How to Pick a Green Place to Stay

Seek certifications such as EarthCheck, Travelife, or Green Tourism.

Support the local economy by booking accommodations at farm stays and guesthouses run by locals.

Choose lodgings with eco-friendly toiletries, sustainable trash management, and energy-efficient heating.

If you're going camping, pick low-impact locations that adhere to the "leave no trace" philosophy.

Farm-to-Table Dining and Local Markets

Devon is the ideal location to embrace sustainable dining because of its reputation for serving up fresh, locally sourced food. Selecting local markets, organic cafes, and farm-to-table eateries helps local farmers and food producers while also lowering your carbon footprint.

Devon's Sustainable Dining Destinations

A farm-to-table eatery dedicated to minimizing food waste, Riverford Field Kitchen (Buckfastleigh) serves seasonal organic produce directly from the farm.

The Seahorse (Dartmouth) is a seafood restaurant that specializes in sustainable fishing methods and serves fish that is sourced ethically.

With a focus on sustainability, The Bull Inn (Totnes) is a zero-waste bar serving locally farmed, organic food.

With a view of the ocean, Gara Rock (South Devon Coast) is an eco-friendly restaurant by the sea that serves locally sourced, fresh food.

The Greatest Farmers' Markets in Devon

Visit the local farmers' markets in Devon for a genuine farm-to-fork experience. There, you can get artisan bread, free-range meats, handcrafted cheeses, and organic veggies.

One of Devon's top marketplaces for fresh seafood, organic produce, and handcrafted preserves is the Exeter Farmers' Market, which takes place on Thursdays.

For locally grown, sustainably produced food and environmentally friendly goods, the monthly Totnes Good Food Market is a must-visit.

The daily Barnstaple Pannier Market is a historic market that sells ethical products, crafts, and fresh local fruit.

Eco-Tip: When shopping at local markets, bring a reusable shopping bag and steer clear of single-use plastics.

Responsible Wildlife Tourism

From seals, dolphins, and seagulls along the coast to wild ponies on Dartmoor, Devon is home to amazing wildlife. To preserve these delicate ecosystems, it is essential to enjoy wildlife interactions in an ethical and responsible manner.

How to Enjoy Devon's Wildlife in a Sustainable Way

Participate in ethical wildlife tours: Seek for companies that adhere to ethical standards, such Devon Wildlife Trust (which offers guided nature walks) or Sea Watch Foundation (which specializes in dolphin spotting).

Watch from a distance: Never try to feed or disturb wildlife, whether you're observing seals in Brixham or otters in the River Otter.

Follow authorized pathways to prevent harming delicate ecosystems in Dartmoor and Exmoor National Parks.

Visit places for conservation. Encourage groups that concentrate on wildlife rehabilitation and conservation education, such as Paignton Zoo and Wildwood Escot.

Top Locations for Ethical Wildlife Observation

Known for its grey seals, basking sharks, and puffins, Lundy Island is a Marine Conservation Zone.

Rare seabirds and breathtaking coastal landscape can be found in Berry Head Nature Reserve (Brixham).

A popular location for rockpooling and education on marine conservation is the Wembury Marine Centre.

Eco-Tip: Select quiet, low-impact wildlife excursions rather than boat tours that harass dolphins or disrupt marine life.

Reducing Your Carbon Footprint While Traveling

Sustainable travel is more than simply where you stay and what you eat; it also involves how you get around and the decisions you make while there.

Devon's Green Transportation Options

Take public transportation: Devon's bus and train system reduces pollution while making transportation simple. Take the picturesque Riviera Line (Exeter to Torbay) or the Tarka Line (Exeter to Barnstaple).

Walk or bike: It's the ideal way to see many of Devon's towns, coasts, and rural paths. An easy and environmentally friendly way to explore is to rent an electric bike.

Carpooling or renting an electric vehicle: If you must drive, Exeter and Plymouth provide electric vehicle rentals.

Other Sustainable Travel Options

Carry a reusable water bottle to help reduce plastic waste, as many Devon towns have free water refill facilities.

Stay longer in one place: To cut down on needless transportation emissions, choose a leisurely travel style and spend more time at one site rather than hurrying between them.

Respect the environment by abiding by the Countryside Code, which calls for not leaving any trash behind, controlling dogs, and showing consideration for wildlife.

Making informed decisions about everything from where you stay and eat to how you explore the area and engage with wildlife is essential to traveling sustainably in Devon.

You may enjoy the finest of Devon while preserving its beauty for future generations by choosing eco-friendly lodging, supporting local companies, and minimizing your environmental impact.

Sustainable tourism in Devon is not only simple, but also a fulfilling and immersive way to experience this breathtaking area, thanks to the abundance of green travel options accessible.

USEFUL INFORMATION

Devon is a friendly place that combines breathtaking natural scenery, historic charm, and contemporary amenities. A comfortable and stress-free trip can be ensured by having practical information, whether you're hiking over moorlands, touring charming beach villages, or enjoying Devonshire cream tea. Everything you need to confidently traverse Devon is included in this section, from emergency contacts and helpful travel applications to currency and tipping norms.

Money, Prices, and Tipping Customs
Money and Modes of Payment

Devon, like the rest of the United Kingdom, uses the British Pound Sterling (£, GBP) as its currency. The denominations of coins are 1p, 2p, 5p, 10p, 20p, 50p, £1, and £2, and the denominations of banknotes are £5, £10, £20, and £50.

The majority of establishments, such as eateries, retail stores, and tourist destinations, take credit and debit cards; the most often used ones are American Express, Visa, and

Mastercard. In addition to mobile payment methods like Apple Pay and Google Pay, contactless payments are readily accessible. While ATMs are widely available in urban areas, access to cash may be restricted in more rural locations. Always have some cash on hand, especially for parking meters, tiny businesses, and rural markets.

Budgeting and Expenses

Devon provides a variety of travel options for a range of price ranges. Budget-conscious tourists can find reasonably priced lodging in tiny guesthouses, hostels, and bed-and-breakfasts. While luxury tourists can take advantage of upscale resorts, private lodges, and spa retreats, mid-range travelers will have a wide variety of cozy hotels, self-catering cottages, and boutique stays to pick from.

There are several affordable places to eat, including bakeries, cafés, and fish and chip stores. While those looking for excellent dining can find upscale restaurants serving gourmet dishes prepared with local, fresh ingredients, mid-range dining options include gastropubs, historic inns, and casual dining establishments.

The cost of transportation varies according to whether you are taking private tours, renting a car, or using public buses and railroads. While museums, castles, and guided tours may charge admission, Devon's beaches, national parks, and ancient towns are among its top attractions, which are all free.

Tipping Culture

Tipping is not often expected in Devon, although it is appreciated. If service is not covered by the bill, it is typical to tip between 10% and 15% in restaurants. Tipping is less popular at cafés and pubs, although it's always polite to leave tiny change or round up the amount. It's customary for cabs to round up to the closest pound or add about 10%. Porters and housekeeping employees at hotels value little gratuities for excellent service.

Healthcare Services and Emergency Contacts
Numbers for Emergencies

For prompt assistance from the police, fire department, ambulance, or coastguard in an emergency, phone 999 (or 112). Dial 101 for non-emergency police assistance.

Medical Care and Drugstores

For medical support, Devon has well-equipped general practitioners (GPs), hospitals, and pharmacies. Dial NHS 111, which offers 24-hour medical help, for non-emergency health advice. In larger places like Exeter and Plymouth, pharmacies are open every day, and some are open twenty-four hours a day.

The Royal Devon and Exeter Hospital in Exeter, Derriford Hospital in Plymouth, and North Devon District Hospital in Barnstaple are among the hospitals that offer accident and emergency (A&E) services. Since not all medications that are available overseas may be available in the UK, travelers should bring any prescription drugs and medications they may need.

Insurance for Travel

Travel insurance, which covers medical costs, travel cancellations, lost luggage, and unforeseen delays, is strongly advised. International tourists should make sure their insurance covers healthcare within the UK, even though UK citizens can use NHS services.

Etiquette and Customs in the Area
In general, etiquette

Devon residents are warm and inviting, and your trip will be more enjoyable if you know some basic etiquette. A typical greeting is "Hello" or "Alright?" The British place a high importance on being courteous, therefore using "please" and "thank you" is crucial. Cutting in line is regarded as impolite, and queuing is treated seriously at ticket desks, stores, and bus stops. Devon locals love to strike up a conversation, especially about the weather, local happenings, or their favorite tourist destinations.

Road etiquette and driving

The UK drives on the left side of the road, so keep that in mind if you're renting a car. Devon's country roads can be quite small, with spaces for passing vehicles. It is important for drivers to be ready to reduce their speed and give way to incoming traffic. There are different speed limits: 30 mph in cities, 60 mph on rural roads, and 70 mph on highways.

Pay-and-display machines are frequently required for parking in towns, so it's important to look for any restrictions on local signage.

Outdoor and Beach Etiquette

Devon's scenery and beaches are stunning, and tourists are urged to respect the environment. When visiting places such as Exmoor and Dartmoor, always bring trash with you, don't disturb wildlife, and stay on designated trails. It's a good idea to verify local regulations as some beaches have seasonal dog restrictions.

Traveler-Friendly Apps and Websites
Applications for Transportation

National Rail Enquiries offers the most recent information on train schedules and ticketing. To check bus routes and buy tickets, download the Stagecoach Bus App. Planning for public transportation and navigation are made easier with Google Maps and Citymapper.

Apps for the weather and outdoors

Accurate predictions for Devon's shifting climate can be found on the Met Office Weather App. Tide Times UK assists in organizing beach trips and hikes along the coast, and AllTrails is great for finding trekking trails in Dartmoor and Exmoor.

Local Data and Reservations

The official tourism website, Visit Devon, provides details on events, lodging options, and attractions. Information about historic landmarks, castles, and nature reserves can be found on the websites of the National Trust and English Heritage.

Food and Dining

While HappyCow assists tourists in finding vegan and vegetarian-friendly restaurants in Devon, OpenTable and Resy enable travelers to reserve tables at well-known restaurants.

Apps for emergencies and health

The NHS 111 Online service helps find local healthcare providers and provides medical information. A highly recommended app, What3Words gives exact position information, which is important in an emergency, particularly in rural or coastal areas.

Make reservations for lodging in advance to guarantee a hassle-free trip, especially during the busy summer months when space is scarce. Because certain rural bus routes are uncommon, it is advisable to verify public transportation timetables beforehand. It's always a good idea to have a lightweight rain jacket because Devon's weather may be unpredictable. Additionally, visitors should be mindful of Devon's laid-back way of life, where things may proceed more slowly than in larger towns.

With these useful tips, you'll be ready to take advantage of all Devon has to offer, from its breathtaking coastlines and undulating landscape to its quaint medieval villages and mouthwatering regional food.

Printed in Dunstable, United Kingdom